WITHDRAWN

Our Enduring Spirit

Our Enduring Spirit

PRESIDENT BARACK OBAMA'S FIRST WORDS TO AMERICA

with illustrations by Greg Ruth

HARPER

An Imprint of HarperCollinsPublishers

My fellow citizens:

I stand here today
humbled

by the task before us,
grateful

for the trust you have bestowed,
mindful

of the sacrifices borne by our ancestors.

Forty-four Americans have now taken the presidential oath.

The words have been spoken during rising tides of *prosperity*

and the still waters of *peace.*

On this day,
we gather because we have chosen
hope over fear,
unity of purpose
over conflict and discord.

The time has come
to reaffirm our enduring spirit;

to choose our better history;

to carry forward that precious gift,

that noble idea

passed on from generation to generation:

the God-given promise that

all are equal, *all* are free, and *all* deserve a chance

to pursue their full measure of happiness.

Our journey has never been one of shortcuts or settling for less.

It has not been the *path* for the fainthearted—

for those who prefer leisure over work,

or seek only the pleasures of riches and fame.

Rather, it has been the *risk takers*,
the *doers*,
the *makers of things*—
some celebrated, but more often men and women obscure in their labor—
who have carried us up the long, rugged path towards prosperity and freedom.

For us,

they packed up their few worldly possessions

and traveled across oceans in search of a new life.

For us,

they toiled in sweatshops and settled the West,

endured the lash of the whip and plowed the hard earth.

For us,

they fought and died

in places like Concord

and Gettysburg,

Normandy

and Khe Sanh.

Time and again

these men and women

struggled

and sacrificed

and worked

till their hands were raw

so that we might live a better life.

They saw America as

bigger

than the sum of our individual ambitions,

greater

than all the differences of birth or wealth or faction.

This is the journey we continue today.

Starting today,

we must pick ourselves up,

dust ourselves off,

and begin again the work of remaking America.

For everywhere we look, there is work to be done.

We know

that our patchwork heritage is a *strength,*

not a weakness.

We are a nation of Christians and Muslims,

Jews and Hindus

and nonbelievers.

We are shaped by every language and culture,

drawn from every end of this Earth.

It is ultimately the *faith* and *determination*

of the American people upon which this nation relies.

It is the *kindness*

to take in a stranger when the levees break,

the *selflessness* of workers . . .

which sees us through our darkest hours.

It is the firefighter's *courage*

to storm a stairway filled with smoke,

but also a parent's *willingness*

to nurture a child that finally decides our fate.

Our challenges may be new.

The instruments with which we meet them may be new.

But those values upon which our success depends—

honesty and hard work,

courage and fair play,

tolerance and curiosity,

loyalty and patriotism—

these things are old.

These things are true.

This
is the price and the promise of citizenship.

This

is the meaning of our liberty and our creed,

why men and women and children

of every race and every faith

can join in celebration across this magnificent mall;

and why a man whose father less than sixty years ago

might not have been served at a local restaurant

can now stand before you to take a most sacred oath.

So let us mark this day with remembrance
of *who* we are
and *how far* we have traveled.

In the year of America's birth,

in the coldest of months,

a small band of patriots huddled by dying campfires

on the shores of an icy river.

The capital was abandoned.

The enemy was advancing.

The snow was stained with blood.

At a moment when the outcome of our revolution was most in doubt,

the father of our nation ordered these words to be read to the people:

"Let it be told to the future world...
that in the depth of winter,
when nothing but hope and virtue could survive...
that the city and the country,
alarmed at one common danger,
came forth to meet [it]."

America:

In the face of *our* common dangers,

in this winter of *our* hardship,

let us remember these timeless words.

With hope and virtue,

let us *brave* once more the icy currents

and *endure* what storms may come.

Let it be said by our children's children

that when we were tested we *refused* to let this journey end,

that we did not turn back nor did we falter;

and with *eyes fixed on the horizon*

and God's grace upon us,

we carried forth that great gift of freedom

and delivered it safely

to future generations.

Thank you.

God bless you.

And God bless the United States of America.

Illustrator's Note

The thing about Barack Obama that first caught my attention wasn't so much what he said or promised or how he answered an opponent in one of those early primary debates. It was how he listened. Art is mostly about listening, really. The best art comes not when you're yelling outward with your medium but when you're quiet and listening to its source. There was something captivating about how our future president listened, and for the remaining eighteen months of that election season, I listened too.

This book and the whole amazing experience behind it came from a similar place. I had decided, perhaps in a crazy fit, that I was working in the studio too much and beginning to forget to have fun with my time there. When you make your art your work, your source of income, it tends without your even noticing to become, more than anything else, work. Suddenly going into the studio to draw each and every day, as fantastic as it sounds, was becoming drudgery—even though I loved the projects I was working on. So I started something I called the 52 Weeks Project. Each Monday, for a year, I would make a new drawing and post it out to the world. It could be about anything at all. Just for fun.

Needless to say, when Obama won the election, I was out-of-my-tree excited. Like to so many others, it felt to me like something really big had happened; but after a long time of big things happening that were scary and terrible, this was just purely wonderful to me. I was electrified. So when I woke up on that Wednesday, being utterly incapable of doing the work I was supposed to be doing, I started drawing portraits of Obama. Over and over again. I wasn't even paying attention to it really—I was just listening. I started posting them up as an addendum to the normal 52 Weeks Project, and the response was overwhelming: it seemed everyone who followed the project was as excited as I was about what was finally happening. So I just started running. Back and forth between the drawing table and the scanner and the computer—ink-stained hands clattering away to upload images ten at a time. It was like being part of a wave tumbling and crashing over itself—hope, simply put, and powerfully executed.

I got a note from Brenda Bowen at HarperCollins later that day. Also dizzy with the excitement of that day, Brenda thought it should go further: She thought it might be fun to turn these drawings into a book. Already at this point there had been untold numbers of biographies and even children's books about Obama, and I didn't want to pile on. It was Brenda who thought of the idea to illustrate our newly elected president's inaugural address, and I was hooked. It seemed like the perfect match for the excitement and passion and drive I couldn't contain and that I felt all around me.

I hope these feelings come through in the work you hold in your hands. It's too hard to see my work with a clear eye, especially in light of the moment it attempts to illustrate. I can say, though, when I look at these pieces and quiet my mind, I can listen again to that which birthed them. I'm glad for having been here, in this time and in this place, to hear that music and to have danced to such a tune on such a day as this.

Inaugural Address

By President Barack Hussein Obama

My fellow citizens: I stand here today humbled by the task before us, grateful for the trust you've bestowed, mindful of the sacrifices borne by our ancestors.

I thank President Bush for his service to our nation as well as the generosity and cooperation he has shown throughout this transition.

Forty-four Americans have now taken the presidential oath. The words have been spoken during rising tides of prosperity and the still waters of peace. Yet, every so often, the oath is taken amidst gathering clouds and raging storms. At these moments, America has carried on not simply because of the skill or vision of those in high office, but because we, the people, have remained faithful to the ideals of our forebears and true to our founding documents.

So it has been; so it must be with this generation of Americans.

That we are in the midst of crisis is now well understood. Our nation is at war against a far-reaching network of violence and hatred. Our economy is badly weakened, a consequence of greed and irresponsibility on the part of some, but also our collective failure to make hard choices and prepare the nation for a new age. Homes have been lost, jobs shed, businesses shuttered. Our health care is too costly, our schools fail too many—and each day brings further evidence that the ways we use energy strengthen our adversaries and threaten our planet.

These are the indicators of crisis, subject to data and statistics. Less measurable, but no less profound, is a sapping of confidence across our land; a nagging fear that America's decline is inevitable, that the next generation must lower its sights.

Today I say to you that the challenges we face are real. They are serious and they are many. They will not be met easily or in a short span of time. But know this, America: They will be met.

On this day, we gather because we have chosen hope over fear, unity of purpose over conflict and discord. On this day, we come to proclaim an end to the petty grievances and false promises, the recriminations and worn-out dogmas that for far too long have strangled our politics. We remain a young nation. But in the words of Scripture, the time has come to set aside childish things. The time has come to reaffirm our enduring spirit; to choose our better history; to carry forward that precious gift, that noble idea passed on from generation to generation: the God-given promise that all are equal, all are free, and all deserve a chance to pursue their full measure of happiness.

In reaffirming the greatness of our nation, we understand that greatness is never a given. It must be earned. Our journey has never been one of shortcuts or settling for less. It has not been the path for the fainthearted, for those who prefer leisure over work or seek only the pleasures of riches and fame. Rather, it has been the risk takers, the doers, the makers of things—some celebrated, but more often men and women obscure in their labor—who have carried us up the long, rugged path towards prosperity and freedom.

For us, they packed up their few worldly possessions and traveled across oceans in search of a new life. For us, they toiled in sweatshops and settled the West, endured the lash of the whip and plowed the hard earth. For us, they fought and died in places like Concord and Gettysburg, Normandy and Khe Sanh.

Time and again these men and women struggled and sacrificed and worked till their hands were raw so that we might live a better life. They saw America as bigger than the sum of our individual ambitions, greater than all the differences of birth or wealth or faction.

This is the journey we continue today. We remain the most prosperous, powerful nation on Earth. Our workers are no less productive than when this crisis began. Our minds are no less inventive, our goods and services no less needed than they were last week, or last month, or last year. Our capacity remains undiminished. But our time of standing pat, of protecting narrow interests and putting off unpleasant decisions—that time has surely passed. Starting today, we must pick ourselves up, dust ourselves off, and begin again the work of remaking America.

For everywhere we look, there is work to be done. The state of our economy calls for action, bold and swift. And we will act, not only to create new jobs, but to lay a new foundation for growth. We will build the roads and bridges, the electric grids and digital lines that feed our commerce and bind us together. We'll restore science to its rightful place and wield technology's wonders to raise health care's quality and lower its cost. We will harness the sun and the winds and the soil to fuel our cars and run our factories. And we will transform our schools and colleges and universities to meet the demands of a new age. All this we can do. All this we will do.

Now, there are some who question the scale of our ambitions, who suggest that our system cannot tolerate too many big plans. Their memories are short, for they have forgotten what this country has already done, what free men and women can achieve when imagination is joined to common purpose, and necessity to courage. What the cynics fail to understand is that the ground has shifted beneath them, that the stale political arguments that have consumed us for so long no longer apply.

The question we ask today is not whether our government is too big or too small, but whether it works—whether it helps families find jobs at a decent wage, care they can afford, a retirement that is dignified. Where the answer is yes, we intend to move forward. Where the answer is no, programs will end. And those of us who manage the public's dollars will be held to account, to spend wisely, reform bad habits, and do our business in the light of day, because only then can we restore the vital trust between a people and their government.

Nor is the question before us whether the market is a force for good or ill. Its power to generate wealth and expand freedom is unmatched. But this crisis has reminded us that without a watchful eye, the market can spin out of control. The nation cannot prosper long when it favors only the prosperous. The success of our economy has always depended not just on the size of our gross domestic product, but on the reach of our prosperity, on the ability to extend opportunity to every willing heart—not out of charity, but because it is the surest route to our common good.

As for our common defense, we reject as false the choice between our safety and our ideals. Our Founding

Fathers, faced with perils that we can scarcely imagine, drafted a charter to assure the rule of law and the rights of man—a charter expanded by the blood of generations. Those ideals still light the world, and we will not give them up for expedience' sake.

And so, to all the other peoples and governments who are watching today, from the grandest capitals to the small village where my father was born, know that America is a friend of each nation, and every man, woman, and child who seeks a future of peace and dignity. And we are ready to lead once more.

Recall that earlier generations faced down fascism and communism not just with missiles and tanks, but with the sturdy alliances and enduring convictions. They understood that our power alone cannot protect us, nor does it entitle us to do as we please. Instead they knew that our power grows through its prudent use; our security emanates from the justness of our cause, the force of our example, the tempering qualities of humility and restraint.

We are the keepers of this legacy. Guided by these principles once more we can meet those new threats that demand even greater effort, even greater cooperation and understanding between nations. We will begin to responsibly leave Iraq to its people and forge a hard-earned peace in Afghanistan. With old friends and former foes, we'll work tirelessly to lessen the nuclear threat, and roll back the specter of a warming planet.

We will not apologize for our way of life, nor will we waver in its defense. And for those who seek to advance their aims by inducing terror and slaughtering innocents, we say to you now that our spirit is stronger and cannot be broken—you cannot outlast us, and we will defeat you.

For we know that our patchwork heritage is a strength, not a weakness. We are a nation of Christians and Muslims, Jews and Hindus and nonbelievers. We are shaped by every language and culture, drawn from every end of this Earth; and because we have tasted the bitter swill of civil war and segregation, and emerged from that dark chapter stronger and more united, we cannot help but believe that the old hatreds shall someday pass; that the lines of tribe shall soon dissolve; that as the world grows smaller, our common humanity shall reveal itself; and that America must play its role in ushering in a new era of peace.

To the Muslim world, we seek a new way forward, based on mutual interest and mutual respect. To those leaders around the globe who seek to sow conflict or blame their society's ills on the West, know that your people will judge you on what you can build, not what you destroy.

To those who cling to power through corruption and deceit and the silencing of dissent, know that you are on the wrong side of history, but that we will extend a hand if you are willing to unclench your fist.

To the people of poor nations, we pledge to work alongside you to make your farms flourish and let clean waters flow; to nourish starved bodies and feed hungry minds. And to those nations like ours that enjoy relative plenty, we say we can no longer afford indifference to the suffering outside our borders, nor can we consume the world's resources without regard to effect. For the world has changed, and we must change with it.

As we consider the role that unfolds before us, we remember with humble gratitude those brave Americans who at this very hour patrol far-off deserts and distant mountains. They have something to tell us, just as the fallen heroes who lie in Arlington whisper through the ages.

We honor them not only because they are the guardians of our liberty, but because they embody the spirit of service—a willingness to find meaning in something greater than themselves.

And yet at this moment, a moment that will define a generation, it is precisely this spirit that must inhabit us all. For as much as government can do, and must do, it is ultimately the faith and determination of the American people upon which this nation relies. It is the kindness to take in a stranger when the levees break, the selflessness of workers who would rather cut their hours than see a friend lose their job which sees us through our darkest hours. It is the firefighter's courage to storm a stairway filled with smoke, but also a parent's willingness to nurture a child that finally decides our fate.

Our challenges may be new. The instruments with which we meet them may be new. But those values upon which our success depends—honesty and hard work, courage and fair play, tolerance and curiosity, loyalty and patriotism— these things are old. These things are true. They have been the quiet force of progress throughout our history.

What is demanded, then, is a return to these truths. What is required of us now is a new era of responsibility—a recognition on the part of every American that we have duties to ourselves, our nation, and the world; duties that we do not grudgingly accept, but rather seize gladly, firm in the knowledge that there is nothing so satisfying to the spirit, so defining of our character than giving our all to a difficult task.

This is the price and the promise of citizenship. This is the source of our confidence   the knowledge that God calls on us to shape an uncertain destiny. This is the meaning of our liberty and our creed, why men and women and children of every race and every faith can join in celebration across this magnificent mall; and why a man whose father less than sixty years ago might not have been served in a local restaurant can now stand before you to take a most sacred oath.

So let us mark this day with remembrance of who we are and how far we have traveled. In the year of America's birth, in the coldest of months, a small band of patriots huddled by dying campfires on the shores of an icy river. The capital was abandoned. The enemy was advancing. The snow was stained with blood. At the moment when the outcome of our revolution was most in doubt, the father of our nation ordered these words to be read to the people:

"Let it be told to the future world . . . that in the depth of winter, when nothing but hope and virtue could survive . . . that the city and the country, alarmed at one common danger, came forth to meet [it]."

America: In the face of our common dangers, in this winter of our hardship, let us remember these timeless words. With hope and virtue, let us brave once more the icy currents and endure what storms may come. Let it be said by our children's children that when we were tested we refused to let this journey end, that we did not turn back nor did we falter; and with eyes fixed on the horizon and God's grace upon us, we carried forth that great gift of freedom and delivered it safely to future generations.

Thank you. God bless you. And God bless the United States of America.

For Brenda Bowen

Our Enduring Spirit: President Barack Obama's First Words to America
Text copyright © 2009 by Barack Hussein Obama
Illustrations copyright © 2009 by Greg Ruth

Library of Congress Cataloging-in-Publication Data
Obama, Barack.
Our enduring spirit : President Barack Obama's first words to
America / with illustrations by Greg Ruth. — 1st ed.
p. cm.
ISBN 978-0-06-183455-4 (trade bdg.) — ISBN 978-0-06-183456-1 (lib. bdg.)
1. Obama, Barack—Inauguration, 2009—Juvenile literature. 2. Obama, Barack—Oratory—
Juvenile literature. 3. Presidents—United States—Inaugural addresses—Juvenile literature.
4. National characteristics, American—Juvenile literature.
5. United States—Politics and government—2009—Juvenile literature. I. Ruth, Greg, ill. II. Title.
J82.E91 2009a   352.23'860973—dc22   2009014361   CIP   AC

Typography by Rachel Zegar
09 10 11 12 13   CG/WOR   10 9 8 7 6 5 4 3 2 1
❖
First Edition